PRAISE FOR

Avail

"Fans of Marianne Moore and Robyn Schiff will delight in *Avail,* which weaves together stories of the poet's adolescent diagnosis of von Willebrand disease with her mother's breast cancer battle, all while exploring the lives of other women in the arts: Maria Callas, Edith Wharton, and Rita Hayworth, to name just a few. These formally deft, often arch lyrics expand the possibilities of the ekphrastic poem, interrogating how our aesthetic representations of suffering and illness render the true realities of pain invisible. In art, do we avail ourselves to physical suffering, or cast a veil over it? In this stunning and assured first collection, O'Luanaigh shows us how poetry does both."

—Paisley Rekdal, author of *West: A Translation*

"Refracted through the prisms of gender, history, and culture, the poems in *Avail* are as rhapsodic as they are fierce in their reckonings. With both 'a screwball spring / in my step' and an eye on 'the honest falsehood,' Erin O'Luanaigh razes and rebuilds ideas about women's lives, taking on troublesome themes with wry formal panache. From the glamourous artifice of early Hollywood to the broken magnificence of opera, and while presenting accounts of a self moving from girlhood through womanhood, O'Luanaigh is a poet of tender intensity. *Avail* is an exquisite debut."

—Rick Barot, author of *Moving the Bones*

"I want to call this book careful. Also reckless. Measured and wild, brainy and passionate, serious and sparkling with wit. Not only in themselves but in how they speak to and across each other, these lyrics—lined and in prose—weave their impossibly delicate, improbably strong veil, wielding art not only to ornament but also to illuminate experience. Never have I seen such a mature, fully-realized debut."

—Katharine Coles, author of *Time and Chance*

"Erin O'Luanaigh's poems revel in classic Hollywood panache, paying brilliant homage to the femmes fatales in whose snowy VHS flicker the author came of age. Her lines zing and sizzle and smolder, revealing how the deepest love may be masked by the punchiest wit. This is not simply a book of cinephrastic marvels, though. Here, writing is also survival practice and spiritual inquiry. What music avails a woman who outlives a critical childhood illness and then nurses beloved others through their own travails? Recalling Keats's 'vale of Soul-making,' O'Luanaigh's close-up shots with mortality give her insight into the heart's depths and the otherworldliness of creativity, the 'curious strength / of a talent larger than the self.' Resurrected, glittering with life, her language effervescent as a flute of brut champagne, O'Luanaigh is a chanteuse lifting the veil of wonder."

—V. Penelope Pelizzon, author of *A Gaze Hound That Hunteth by the Eye*

"*Avail* shows us a world in which American popular culture mixes and meshes with European high culture, in which sestinas go wild, in which veils become vales, and in which lyric playfulness runs hard against chill form. This is an irrepressible début collection, one to relish time after time."

—Kevin Hart, author of *Wild Track: New and Selected Poems* and *Dark-Land: Memoir of a Secret Childhood*

"Reading and rereading Erin O'Luanaigh's poems—the liveliest, most happening, most electric I've encountered in ages—is like listening to a wiser, jazzier, more versatile incarnation of Don Marquis's Mehitabel the Cat recounting her adventures in this and a dozen past lives. Don't let that lead you to believe that O'Luanaigh is 'toujours gai.' She is a poet of rich moods, infinite notes. Her French motto is rather 'C'est la vie'—that's life, in all its irreducible splendor. She is splendid."

—Boris Dralyuk, author of *My Hollywood and Other Poems*

AVAIL

POEMS

ERIN O'LUANAIGH

Introduction by Ange Mlinko

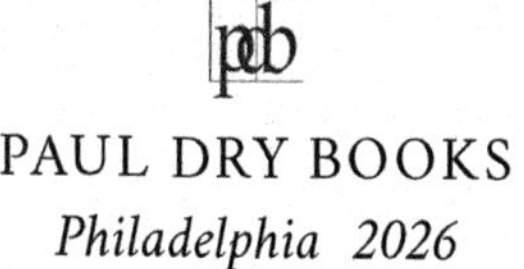

PAUL DRY BOOKS
Philadelphia 2026

First Paul Dry Books Edition, 2026

Paul Dry Books, Inc.
Philadelphia, Pennsylvania
www.pauldrybooks.com

Printed in the United States of America

Library of Congress Control Number: 2025941193

ISBN: 978-1-58988-209-6

for my grandparents,

Donato Barbiero (1927–2016)

& Grace Santagata Barbiero (1931–)

CONTENTS

INTRODUCTION

Ange Mlinko

It's not every day, or every year, that a student steps into your classroom with an encyclopedic knowledge of film, jazz, opera, musical theater, and yes literature, and proceeds to write poems referencing Maria Callas, Barbara Stanwyck, Elizabeth Taylor, and other showbiz legends; the Roman vestal virgins; the Biblical Salomé; Princess Di; Madonna. But that's how I met Erin O'Luanaigh, and I was lucky.

Erin is one in an impressive line of writers and artists (Robert Louis Stevenson, Joan Murray, Joni Mitchell, H.G. Wells, and Saul Bellow come to mind) who survived the bedridden tedium and horror of a childhood illness by immersing themselves in books. In our poet's case, she also had a family of film aficionados to provide her with classic American movies during her convalescence. As she regained her health, she threw herself into vocal training and theater; her identification with the heroines of the silver screen was complete, as she illustrates in "Snow," where an exhausted VCR tape gives out and the TV glass captures her ghostly outline:

> . . . a pixelated
> ice age, Stanwyck snowing tears
> even as she smiles,
>
> and me, rewinding
> the melting tape to the point
> of dissolution,
>
> whiting out each scene
> with a love that, like all love,
> distorts its object,

glazes it with ice,
swallows it like a mailbox
in a mounting heap,

until the tape stops
and only my face, bloodless,
winters the blank screen.

"Snow" opens *Avail* and initiates a series of reflections that feature recurring motifs: white and red, or pallor and sanguinification (a diagnosis of a blood disease will emerge); femininity and martyrdom; the screwball comedienne on screen (performative) and her heartbreak off screen (sacrificial); singing as a refined form of screaming; family (a further extension of "blood") as a form that holds a life together at the cost of continually breaking apart. Intermittently weaving through these themes, or holding them transparently together like a peritoneum, is the veil: a quintessential female garment, metonym for both the bride and the nun, revelation and concealment.

Thus "avail," whose modern definition—an intransitive verb meaning "to be useful, helpful, or effective in accomplishing a purpose; to be effectual; to serve; to be of use or assistance"—shades into its archaic, now obsolete usage:

> To descend; to come, go, or get down; to dismount, alight. To sail down stream, or away on an ebb tide. To lower oneself, submit, yield. To lower (the visor of a helmet), to uncover; *hence*, to take off, doff (hat, cap, etc.). To degrade, abase, humble; to lower. (Oxford English Dictionary)

Both "veil" and "avail" are expressions of an aesthetic: for instance, that poetry is veiled language ("I took up for banter, wisecracks, deep emotion / veiled in ironic distance," as the poem "Marriage" puts it). Language itself is less than gossamer, as Edmund Burke among others recognized: his definition of poetry, "the art of substantiating shadows, and of lending existence to nothing" is uncannily similar to *A Midsummer Night's Dream*: "to give to airy nothing / a local habitation and a name."

But isn't poetry also written in blood? Elsewhere in our Shakespeare, in the Sonnets, we read: "Thence comes it that my name receives a brand, / And almost thence my nature is subdu'd / To what it works in, like the dyer's hand." (Erin and I read W.H. Auden's *The Dyer's Hand* together in a tutorial.) Blood is what dyes her sheets when the disease first presents itself; symbolically, she turns it into ink; thus she avails herself of the poetic tradition.

This brings us to the deepest aspect of her ars poetica, related to the archaic definition of avail: a descent. The Greek word for this is *katabasis,* and it describes a journey into the Underworld, à la Persephone. *Avail* is just such a katabasis, replete with pomegranate-red stains. With this in mind, one must read "Snow" as an updated version of Demeter's daughter, trapped in Hades all winter until she can be reunited with her mother in spring.

What's the point of katabasis? To quiz the dead, of course; it's a form of intelligence-gathering, as evidenced by Odysseus's descent in Book XI of *The Odyssey,* or Aeneas's in Book VI of *The Aeneid.* Some of the personages they met were fellow warriors, others were kin. In *Avail,* many of the personages we meet are dead women—warriors of a sort, like Judy Garland, aka Frances Gumm; Irene Dunne; St. Catherine; Helen Frankenthaler. The wheels they are broken on are mentioned almost in passing; it's not their martyrdom that features in the poems, but their ardor, which gets passed on like a torch to women like our author, who accepts it with a quip. "My hair grew to pre-Raphaelite proportions," she writes in "Oxford" (another figure of katabasis) "teased by dampness and excessive thought." It's the light touch that strikes the reader in conjunction with the serious subject matter: this is addressed outright in "The Swing," where chiaroscuro depths lurk in even the lushest Fragonard, and mirth in the darkest places likewise. It's no wonder that the end of the poem—"they . . . never saw the wheels' gritted teeth / beneath her faux /

Rococo"—calls back to the previous poem, in which St. Catherine is identified in paintings by the presence of that medieval torture instrument.

Other figures we meet in O'Luanaigh's underworld haven't met grisly deaths by wheel or barbiturate, but appear to us as the minor arcana of twentieth-century celebrities in idyllic, palm-tree settings:

> . . . I walk him by the canal
> that runs its concrete vein through Scottsdale,
> feeds the pool at the Arizona Biltmore,
> where once, in a deck chair,
>
> Irving Berlin dreamt up "White Christmas"
> over a Tequila Sunrise . . .
>
> ("The Phoenicians")

> . . . or further up, where once lived Brecht,
> Adorno, Schoenberg, and the magic Mann
> (all told: the Weimar by the Sea) in glass-decked
> houses out of David Hockney, we list,
> *verklempt*, out of the Villa's gate. The novelist,
> when not apprising Hesse of his wanton lawn
>
> (the Eden in which he'd torment Leverkühn),
> partied with Cagney, Jack Warner, Berlin,
> and handed *tassen* to a young Sontag, soon
> to take the devil's bargain for her own art.
>
> ("Pacific Palisades")

There's a secret link between these personages and the family drama that plays out across the collection: they're all "transplants . . . like the palm trees" that "live in an invented place, / precarious as language."

Odysseus meets his mother, Aeneas his father in the Underworld; the figure that our narrator most wants to see on her journey is her beloved grandfather (her mother's father) who nursed her during her illness and fostered her passion for movies. She elaborates in her verse-essay, "Avail:"

> Sometimes I think I see him on the street. Once I followed a man in Boston for five extra blocks, just to be sure. They wore the same coat, had the same gait. I was just waiting for the right time to surprise you, he might say. Did you ever think I'd really leave you?

The katabasis culminates in a voyage to Italy, specifically Naples, ancestral homeland on her mother's side; as if that weren't sufficiently symbolic (see Naples and die, said Goethe), it is also the place where an ampoule of the blood of St. Januarius (third century A.D.) is housed. Three times a year, the faithful gather in the basilica to witness the miracle of its liquefaction, a fitting image for the poet's own (now manageable) clotting disorder.

A further curiosity: in Naples, she books a stay in the building where the 1954 Vittorio de Sica film (and Sophia Loren vehicle), *The Gold of Naples,* was filmed. Something has come full circle: the little girl at the beginning of *Avail* has by the end broken the fourth wall, after a fashion: she has entered the reel (the real!); she is, indeed, a sequel, and anticipates further sequels in a revelation of the interchangeability of life and art: "The end / of my world is the beginning of yours."

Gainesville, FL, April 2025

AVAIL

"and with delicate woven cloths covered her up well"

—Sappho

Snow

It drifts and it drifts
as the finished VHS
respools its tinsel,

white bands flurrying
across the glossy hilltop
of the TV screen.

A modern weather
(like the swirl of asbestos
in Dorothy Gale's

ear, the Ivory Soap
flakes strewn over Bedford Falls,
the sprayable foam),

it mocks the snap-pop
of a stand of trees buckling
under a blanket,

or a bucket's ice-
shell cracking above the heat
of the tape's firelog.

Its storm will kick up
when I replay the movie—
a grocery aisle

now edged with blizzards,
anklets coated in hoarfrost,
summers forecasting

a pixelated
ice age, Stanwyck snowing tears
even as she smiles,

and me, rewinding
the melting tape to the point
of dissolution,

whiting out each scene
with a love that, like all love,
distorts its object,

glazes it with ice,
swallows it like a mailbox
in a mounting heap,

until the tape stops
and only my face, bloodless,
winters the blank screen.

A Childhood Illness

They began with the Christmas tree, which went up a few days before Halloween. Presents two weeks into November. Then a birthday party on Thanksgiving, though I wouldn't turn thirteen for another three months, and on Christmas, an Easter egg hunt. And she can't miss the Fourth of July, they said. That's her favorite. So we had a barbeque on New Year's Day, combined with a 7th grade graduation ceremony. I held a diploma warm from the printer in one hand, a hotdog in the other. What a lovely ceremony, they said, snapping Polaroids and sticking them, gray, into silver photo albums. Someone drove up in a blue convertible with a bow on the hood. It's yours, they said. Don't bother with thank-you notes. And they snapped pictures of me in a graduation gown over a big puffer coat, sitting in the passenger seat, waving an American flag. We've done everything we could, they said when the party was over. There's nothing left to do. So they waited. A quiet week passed, then two, then three. And when I lived, I was embarrassed. I felt I'd let them down.

Cover Girl

It was a hospital season, a grainy black-and-white reel—
exam rooms, waiting rooms, offices, hallways,
my northwest-facing bedroom, my closed eyes—
until the day you took me to the movies, a Friday morning,
and I, the only child in a throng of gray ("Why aren't you
in school?"), sat by you, holding tightly to your arm,
and watched the whole bright world come roaring in, alive.

"So red, so red," I sighed in the ice-cream parlor afterward
over her glorious Technicolor hair, her lips, her piked fingernails,
as we savored our usuals—pistachio (yours)
and black raspberry (mine)—at our blue window-booth,
while outside, the pumpkins smiled back at me,
and the sunburnt leaves died floridly on the vine.

For Frances Gumm

She roared and stamped her feet
in the wings of Carnegie Hall
under the cover
of the overture (who else
had their own overture?),
then did it in a film
because it seemed
like something she might do.

Mouth open in the mode
of the permanently-dumbstruck,
she believed in love poems, the Kennedys,
and the efficacy of tears.
For months, she thought
her studio-appointed sentry
was her closest female friend.

An invitation to pity
(poor little thing!),
she broke on top notes,
forgot lyrics
so every song would have
its own comeback story.
Softening to parody and drug-haze,
she was dropped by CBS
because she looked too desperate
and touched her guests too much.

Still, the curious strength
of a talent larger than the self—
as, say, in the after-hours nightclub
of *A Star is Born*,

when the chairs were upended
on tables, the band
was milling around,
and she moved in and out
of pools of light.

His Girl Friday

She loves him in a loathsome sort of way,
gives one last sigh for life in Albany,
and at the fade, decides that she will stay.

He fixed it so she couldn't get away,
played his Svengali act for comedy.
She loves him in a loathsome sort of way.

He jammed the presses, framed her fiancé
with phony dough, a tawdry mashing spree—
but by the fade, she knows that she will stay.

He trotted out every newsroom cliché:
"For truth! For freedom of the press! For me!"
She loves him in a loathsome sort of way.

Their bickering is, after all, just play.
She shows her decoy lover to a taxi
before the fade. She knew that she would stay.

When lust settles down, hate saves the day;
divorce can cure a marriage's ennui.
She loves him in a loathsome sort of way,
and at the fade, admits that she will stay.

Marriage

Nearly Christmas. I'd trotted out my gold-rimmed
Nick and Nora glasses (the better to see you with)

and mixed myself a holiday martini (cranberries, juice,
orange liqueur). You'd recently given up drinking.

On screen, a template for happiness: gin, then icepack
on a constant loop, desire preserved by the fog

of a saturnalian stupor, by wit, by the casting of
a snappy, self-sufficient terrier where a baby should be.

Powell pointed to a spot on Loy's shirt and caught
her retroussé nose; she batted his head mid-swig.

I half-swooned at the intimacy. You shrugged.
(Your love, of the *Vertigo* variety, still languished

in its mirror stage.) "That's your idea of romance?"
"No, marriage." You argued for idealization, fantasy,

spoke of the night you first saw me in *that* dress
(slinky, widow-black), singing "You Belong to Me."

I took up for banter, wisecracks, deep emotion
veiled in ironic distance, an enterprise of both "liberty

and union." Still, when I placed the last champagne-
colored bauble on the tree, aglow, you asked me.

In the fizz of my glass, two cranberries knocked together,
then apart, like plump halves of a broken heart.

The Awful Truth

Nothing is less logical than the truth,
so Irene Dunne and Cary Grant break up
for now. Soon enough they'll learn the truth—
he about her singing teacher (the truth
there is hardly awful) and she about herself
(which is, perhaps, the most awful of truths)—
that she can't live without a man who, truth
be told, loves her best. When he crashes her singing
teacher's apartment and finds her singing
La Serenata, he figures out this truth.
Before long, they'll be off to Connecticut.
Will love conquer all in Connecticut?

It does when, also in Connecticut,
I replay the film. To tell you the truth,
I watch too many movies in Connecticut—
sometimes three a day. Connecticut
is the Arcadia where couples who break up
in rom-coms come to reconnect. I cut
the movies slack (has anyone been to Connecticut?),
but not even real-life Cary Grant himself,
the paragon of romantic love itself,
could win an ex-wife back in Connecticut.
Only movie-Cary can, who hears singing
when he wins Irene, that movie-magic singing.

Out of the city, after nights of singing,
I'm retreating again to Connecticut
to watch a few more movies . . . *Singin'*
in the Rain, or *20,000 Years in Sing Sing*,

but I always return to *The Awful Truth.*
My favorite gag: when the Southern gal sings
"My Dreams are Gone with the Wind" and, as she sings,
a wind effect beneath the stage rakes up
her skirt. Later, Irene will mend her breakup
by trying the same crass trick, singing
the same song at a fancy party—not as herself,
but as Cary's fake sister. (They see themselves

out.) What I wouldn't give for her glinty self-
confidence—not the false courage I summon to sing
when I become a chanteuse version of myself
(a persona borrowed from the record shelf
of a dusty basement in Connecticut).
To shake life by the martini (but stay self-
possessed), to star in the movie of myself
instead of playing second lead . . . the Ruth
Hussey, the Gail Patrick. In *The Awful Truth,*
it's Aunt Patsy, a woman who calls herself
an old tennis ball, bouncing from one breakup
to the next until the ball breaks down . . .

Did I mention my recent breakup?
Forgive me for feeling sorry for myself—
I suppose by watching movies about breakups
I'm salting the wound of my own breakup.
But then, every weekend I go on singing
where he and I met. Avoiding movie breakups
seems futile when you're crying off your makeup
under stage lights. At least in Connecticut
I can escape to the back-lot Connecticut,
to Aunt Patsy's cottage with its broken
locks, which waits to reconcile me to the truth—
that life is too unlike *The Awful Truth.*

The thought's enough to shelve *The Awful Truth*
for another time, another bad breakup.
Perhaps possessed by Irene Dunne herself,
I return to the city, a screwball spring
in my step, nodding fondly to Connecticut.

Avail

To veil

To say *no*. To cover the body. To hide the body. To prevent the gaze of the other. To forbid the gaze of the other. To guard the body as precious. To mark oneself as holy. To gather unto oneself. To store up one's resources. To set a boundary. To construct a barrier for the body. To sketch an outline of the body. To provide a negative image of my body. To hint at what lies beneath by limning the body's shape. To suggest. To tease. To torture by withholding the body. To mark a potential availability. To imply a future unveiling. To signify *yes* by saying *no*.

*

To avail

To say *yes*. To see a value. To explore a possibility. To take the opportunity. To make use of. To respond to generosity. To accept an overture. To help oneself. To satisfy oneself. To have one's fill. To consume. To gorge oneself. To press an advantage. To exploit. To strong-arm. To throw one's weight around. To take what is there for the taking. To pillage. To breach. To cross the barrier erected by another. To unveil. To destroy. To force a retreat. To colonize. To procure another's *no*.

Self-portrait in a bridal veil

At five, I went through a phase of bride-mania. I would hold one of my grandmother's potted plants and walk down the hallway singing the Wedding March, ordering my younger brother to hold out the back of my shirt. When asked whom I was marrying, I would shout, "No one!" or sometimes, "Myself!" I wore a dishtowel on my head.

That year, I went as a bride for Halloween. I wore a ready-made outfit off a supermarket costume rack marked "Bride—Child." The set included a veil that looked like a Vegas showgirl's loincloth. It was a thick, white elastic band with a strip of sequins irregularly glued to it, and from the front and back hung two narrow sheets of tulle.

On Halloween night, the temperature dipped below freezing, and I was forced to wear a sweatsuit beneath my gown. There is a picture of me in a white monstrosity of polyester, stretched tight over a gray OshKosh sweatshirt. I am pouting beneath my veil.

The flammeum

The *flammeum* ("flame-colored") veiled the Roman bride from head to toe. It served to shield her from the eyes of onlookers and, in turn, blind her to the evil spirits and omens that might otherwise plague her on her wedding day.

The Roman bride was said to be "clouded over with a veil." From the verb *nubere* ("to cover or veil oneself for a bridegroom"), Romans extracted the noun *nubes,* meaning "cloud." *Nubes* is the origin of the English word "nubile." A nubile (or marriageable) woman is thus, etymologically-speaking, cloudy or veiled.

*

Cumulonimbus velum

An "accessory" cloud draped over or wrapped around the "parent" cumulonimbus. The velum may look like a veil on the head of a woman, a ring on a finger, a hula-hoop around a torso.

Bedsheets

The hair at the nape of my neck is damp; my sheets feel slick. I've been sleeping for too long, a deep sleep, a dead sleep. It must be late. Somewhere my mother is calling me. She sees my face, pale on the pillow, and comes closer. Time to get up, she's saying, but she still sounds far away. Are you alright? Are you alright? Then a rush of cold air as she pulls away the blanket. The sheets painted to my body, stage-curtain red.

*

Womb

The mother is the first veil.

Great-great grandmother

Part photograph, part hand-painted print, reassembled and restored after going to pieces in an aunt's photo album, she is fuzzy, disjointed, uncanny. One eye glints perceptively from out of a white-washed face, the other lacks sclera or iris, like a brown bead in the head of a teddy bear. And her nose must be a fiction—it is not in the family catalogue, but pinched to vanishment in the bridge and half-snubbed at the end. The storied details have eroded from the top of her gown, which now shows blank, like the aproned uniform of a Harvey Girl. But her veil, high atop a pile of black hair and issuing from a mass of blurry flowers, arcs wide as an umbrella, brushing the tips of her elbows with delicate, banded lace.

*

Veins

The circulatory system is a veil our body has swallowed whole. Its tatting knots around the heart, the lungs, the brain as if tied beneath an old woman's chin. It weaves its blue threads through the tissues of our extremities, ending in the frills of fingers, the furbelows of toes.

The Lady Eve

Barbara Stanwyck sits in a cab, about to join a party at the Connecticut mansion of Henry Fonda's Charles Pike, who knows Stanwyck as Jean Harrington, notorious con artist and card shark. Without taking the trouble to alter her appearance, Jean has adopted the persona of Eve Sidwich, an English aristocrat who just happens to look exactly like Jean. This is the brilliance of her plan; had she dyed her hair, changed her eyebrows, or donned a false nose, Charles might've been suspicious. But because Eve bears such an uncanny resemblance to Jean, Charles is convinced she is not the same dame.

Still, in the cab, she clutches her veil about her face for a moment—nervously, perhaps, or out of a subliminal desire to affect a sudden transformation. As she walks through the door of Charles's mansion, she is still wearing the veil, closed with one fist over her chin. But in the next shot, she has divested herself of it, and stands on the threshold of the drawing room in the naked guise of Eve.

Palatal velum

The soft palate. The veil of unboned tissue at the roof of the mouth which extends from the palatum durum, or hard palate, to the uvula. Consonants formed on the soft palate are called velar consonants. Examples include the voiced velar nasal consonant ŋ (ng as in "sing"). The soft palate lifts when one is singing.

*

Availing myself

In my bedroom, its walls papered with an underwater scene, its bedspread ocean blue, its dresser covered in shells, I have suddenly and all at once outgrown my childhood. I live in its husk, sloughed off overnight, and am being administered something for the pain.

A TV is installed in my room to keep me company. It has a built-in VCR, and in the evenings, my grandfather brings a few taped offerings. In the dark, I wish I was Barbara Stanwyck, Bette Davis, Jean Harlow, imagine myself in glamorous and romantic scenes on a cruise ship, in Brazil, on Park Avenue. In the morning, when my mother enters with the pills that will put me to sleep, I brace for the deluge of new dreams.

In the Morgan Library

The slim captives behind the lattice cage
peer out from a world of steel and Pullman cars,
of red damask, slightly singed by lit cigars,
of the marble, oak, and gilding of the age.

After a trip to Edith Wharton's Mount,
my week's assumed an accidental theme—
as if I arrived in a cloud of ermine and steam,
and you, perhaps escaping some Polish count,

met me for a turn about these shelves
and news of the Van der Luydens or Lily Bart,
as we study the Gutenberg, the *objets d'art*
of noble provenance. Our fantasy selves

have nothing on the one constructed here:
the Tudor tapestry above the fireplace,
the honeycomb vault of famous men encased
in roundels and lunettes lend a veneer

of eminence to Morgan's *nouveau* riches,
as do his volumes from the French (Montaigne,
Voltaire, Balzac, the Fables of La Fontaine
with the frog who puffs up bigger than his britches),

manuscripts from Amsterdam and Venice,
and German philosophers kept under glass.
To ransack Europe is to purchase class:
Wharton built a French chateau in Lenox,

Morgan, born in Connecticut, died in Rome.
We two—Isabel Archers, Daisy Millers—
speechless with splendor, pass through the pillars
that shoulder the foyer's Raphaelite dome

and onto Madison, into the present cold.
We search for a bar to soften the chill
of our own delusions (and a mounting bill),
old-fashioneds in our tumblers glinting gold.

Red Travels

after Helen Frankenthaler

The gesture is the road through a painting, the transcription of movement, the transfer of goods across state lines from Nothing to Being and back, so that the artist comes to see the world as a series of roads. The tractor-lanes dividing the variegated crops. The alleys between the rows of sunflowers. The dock on Lake Michigan that surges up the horizon like a ramp. The creek, the waterfall slicing a dell. The bands of a rainbow. The rust-red bands of the Badlands, veining waves of sandstone. The flutes of Devils Tower with two men climbing, climbing in their separate lanes. A cargo train of blue and yellow cars, like a toy train ringing the hills, like a train of thought. Like taking the sleeper and waking up in a new world. Like Manifest Destiny. Like the tunnel blasted through a mountainside. Like the Shoshone Dam, a path blocked as it was forged. Like the congested rings around Yellowstone that trace its smoking caldera with little white vans. Like the causeway of the Great Salt Lake, bisecting the red from the green. Like the interstate highway system—great destroyer—that is no place at all, but merely the vantage point from which to survey a country, like the canvas on the floor beneath your hand.

Lady in a Fur Wrap

El Greco's women wave
like tubemen in used car lots,
flappable and jelly-eyed
on a cloud or in Toledo.

But here is scrupulosity.
She could be exiting a taxi
in front of the Algonquin.
Her name is Liz or Jen.

St. Catherine's Wheel

Iconographers, great or amateur,
        painted a thousand martyrs:

fair or preternatural,
        banderoled or unspoken,

line-drawn or ghost-limbed,
        resting their arms upon

a wagon wheel or spiked hula-hoop,
        a sock-ring or sun-dial,

the head of a weed-whacker
        or a deadly arc of cake.

If we know her, it is only by
        the broken pattern of its shape.

The Swing

after Fragonard

Jejune profiterole
in a pre-fab pastoral
as rustic as a butterfly tattoo—
there she flew

over my roommate's desk
like a goddess of excess,
blessing all that lay below: a scarved lamp
dampening

the room in boudoir haze,
Gucci bags, a frilly "chaise"
on which she'd lay out pink nightgowns and lie,
who knows why,

about her age (my room-
mate, that is). The bloom
could never come off that rose—its genus,
like Venus,

bred from some soggy myth
that grew to a labyrinth
of fad diets, couture, Audrey Hepburn
films (she yearned

for her tiara'd twee),
and countless *petits-amis*—
all Ivy legacies with fat trust funds
who succumbed

to the lilt of her skirt,
ruffling their polo shirts
pink with desire. (Meanwhile, I got the boot.)
                Not astute,

let us say, they never guessed
that she was cleverer
than they, never saw the wheels' gritted teeth
                beneath her faux
                                Rococo.

Skyscrapers

Our ugliness is beside the point, our inhumanity pleases for its own sake. What use, in fact, is pleasure? What use the trellis or parterre, except to trim the aesthete's lapel? No, we are not your Georgian terraces, as wide and columned as cakes, we are not your cow-eyed Victorian manors, your Federalist squares, your Queen Anne's quoins, your golden-ratioed minarets, turrets, bell-towers, or dreaming Gothic spires . . . We have no use for rustication, for vermiculation, for cornice or pediment, for dog-tooth, bead-and-reel, or egg-and-tongue, for frieze, for mullions with their ball-flowers, for scroll, gargoyle, acanthus, or rosette, we of the steel frame, the bundled tube, the concrete slab, the virtue of size, the pissing contest with the clouds, the iron cage, the cold hard facts, the powers that be, the blank slate, the eyeless needle.

Oxford

after *The Portrait of a Lady*

My hair grew to Pre-Raphaelite proportions,
teased by dampness and excessive thought.
So, too, my sentences, which lengthened beyond
all hope of comprehension, fertilized by James's daft, prolapsed
constructions
such that I "exchanged for a knowledge which was sometimes a
limitation
a presentiment which proved usually to have been a blank."
I shrank under the load, like a William Morris wallflower
in the jungle-stacks of the Bodley, or a fuzzy little creature
scurrying beneath the fan-vault canopies of cathedrals,
studying memorial brasses on the forest floor.

High Culture

Her fake majolica
brimming with moral fables
(the pelican of piety,
a lion ponderously tangled
in "Ave Maria"'s

golden script, the lambs
with their crosscut vexilla)
make a gradual *conquista*
of tabletops and shelves. Reverted
years ago to a faith

that loves a hoarder, she
buys ersatz antiquities
as if preponderance breeds grace,
props them on display stands—serving plates,
carafes, and bowls staggered

like mosaicked peacocks
with antimony eyespots—
enshrines them like they're bona fide,
not mailed from SoCal Renaissance fairs
in crates lined with the *Times*,

as were her icon bread
stamps, her "German" cookie molds
depicting the Crucifixion
(sorrowful treat). A miracle, then,
each time she pulls them down

and plates a meal, heaping
meat sauce on the backs of saints,
mopping Mary's brow, pouring tea
from the mouth of an aquamanile
that is the mouth of God.

Pacific Palisades

It's California: we've reached the end of taste.
We're strolling on the Getty Villa's bluff,
its merit weighed against the megalithic waste
of historic reproduction. (What's Egyptian
about the Egyptian Revival; Parisian
in the Vegas Strip's Arc de Triomphe?)

A super-sized riff on the Villa dei Papyri
("The original, at least, was blown to ash,"
we console ourselves beneath a marquee
hawking lattes) with a lobby built to recall
an excavation, its galleries house the haul
of the thinking man's robber baron: a cache

of Herakleses, kouri, hydra'd hydrias,
a replica of a Pompeii fountain mapped
with West-Coast shells, the coinage of Illyria,
Cycladic figures, the alleged "Mazarin" Venus,
gardens with herbs of ancient Roman genus,
a satyr reclining as in a Kardashian snap . . .

Visitors pose so thickly in the peristyles,
we struggle to escape another's selfie;
still, in an atrium frisbeed with sundials,
I admit equal beguilement by counterfeit
and bona fide alike: "Who's to say what's legit?
A Roman original is a Greek man's copy."

*

Called back from antiquity to the traffic
rumbling below, where mention of Inceville's
studio passes for ancient history (its epics:

Civilization—widely deemed low brow—
and *The Italian*, whose hero nosed the prow
of a gondola down Venice Beach's rills),

or further up, where once lived Brecht,
Adorno, Schoenberg, and the magic Mann
(all told: the Weimar by the Sea) in glass-decked
houses out of David Hockney, we list,
verklempt, out of the Villa's gate. The novelist,
when not apprising Hesse of his wanton lawn

(the Eden in which he'd torment Leverkühn),
partied with Cagney, Jack Warner, Berlin,
and handed *tassen* to a young Sontag, soon
to take the devil's bargain for her own art.
We quote her missive on allusion, that no part
of any work is new, that all is reproduction . . .

Across the highway, we sink through coastal sage
to watch the sunset on the "proper" shore
against outcrops dated to the Miocene Age.
Like good Easterners, we shield our eyes
from the vulgarity of pleasure, the paradise
unearned, the honest falsehood, the easily-adored.

Avail

(continued)

Now, Voyager

In *Now, Voyager,* Bette Davis's Charlotte Vale flees from a domineering mother to board a South-American cruise, her transformation from frump to fashion-plate highlighted in a slow tracking shot of her figure as she stands at the top of a gangplank. The camera takes in her two-toned high-heels, her chic suit, and finally her wide-brimmed hat, orbited by a thin tissue of a veil—meant, no doubt, to symbolize the defenses she has yet to abandon before she can fall in love. But the man for whom she finally falls is married; one night, she kisses him through a veil.

*

Slip

The slip is a form of the veil—a body-veil. It skims Jean Harlow in *Dinner at Eight,* clings to Elizabeth Taylor in *Butterfield 8.* The figure 8 suggests the female form, as a veil.

Invasive lobular carcinoma

A form of breast cancer which often goes undetected by mammograms because of the dispersal of its cancerous cells. Rather than accumulating in a single mass, it spreads its salt-grain tumors in a stroma through the patient's breast. On an MRI screen, invasive lobular carcinoma appears as a white cloud or veil occluding a swath of the breast tissue. In an ultrasound, the cancerous hypoechoic tissue shows black, like a storm cloud darkening the dappled white and gray pattern of the breast, or a mourning veil.

*

The veil of sleep

My mother naps on the recliner and I monitor her breathing, pull the blanket up around her, wonder if she is dreaming and of what. The nap hour is the loneliest one, when I am shut out, must reckon with the sudden silence, the uncertainty, the inability to ask my usual questions:

"Are you too hot? Too cold?"

"What can I make you?"

"Would you please eat something?"

"Are you in pain?"

"Where does it hurt?"

"How many painkillers do you need?"

I fill the hour by growing anxious over the proper time to wake her. Too early and I will have robbed her of sufficient rest; too late and she'll be wide awake at bedtime. (It's easy to overdraw from the bank account of sleep.) I watch her. She shifts suddenly, so I resolve to touch her arm and whisper, "Mom." Still, she jumps. She later tells me that she dreamt of me sitting beside her, watching her.

A film is a veil

Every day, my grandfather sat beside me as I slept. He would bring me stacks of VHS tapes recorded from TCM, labeled along the edge in his "chicken-scratch" handwriting: *Red Dust, The Letter, Ball of Fire, Cover Girl.* When I woke, he would tell me stories of the first time he had seen this or that film, ask me what I thought of this or that actor. I would put in requests for more Bette, more Barbara, more Rita. He would watch them with me until it got too late, humor me as I rewound the magnetic tape over and over, trying to take in every moment of a meaningful scene, pausing a frame to capture the gradations of a gesture or smile, the magic imprinted in the celluloid. He would rest his heavy hand on my head, his fingertips at my temple, subtly checking my pulse.

Velum [mycology]

The white, opaque, web-like membrane that covers the cap and stem of newborn mushrooms, affecting a veiled appearance. In a forest or field, a child might imagine that such a mushroom is a beekeeper, a careful gardener, or a delicate lady on safari.

*

Great grandmother

An unlikely style for a meek Italian girl: the flapper bride. Her knee-length dress is usurped in the front by a floral profusion twice as wide as she is, covered in back by a cathedral-long bank of tulle. Attached to her Juliet cap in two enormous, jagged rosettes, the veil falls, hits the floor, and runs for three more feet before the photograph expires. The white roses in her arms, too, have their own veil: a rain of silver-white streamers that brush her toes. Her face in profile is a Walter Crane illustration of an exquisite captive in a fairy tale.

Salomé

In Oscar Wilde's play, she dances the pseudo-historical Dance of the Seven Veils. Veiling and availing are collapsed. John the Baptist is beheaded by a stripper.

*

Rita Hayworth

She had red hair and red lips and red fingernails and glowing red cheeks—in short, she was aflame with vitality. In musicals, she danced with a vigor that suggested an overabundance of good health, as if she had too much and wanted to get rid of some.

One night, I watched *Salomé,* in which she danced the Dance of the Seven Veils for Charles Laughton's Herod with a fervor almost spasmodic. Her veils were voluminous and multi-colored. The first was a midnight blue full-body veil with gold embroidery that trailed on the floor behind her. She held her arms above her head so that the veil cleared her makuta and screened her face with a shimmer of blue-gold and desire. Desire for what? To keep living, I assume. To flaunt her vitality in the face of John the Baptist, sentenced to death. To flaunt it in mine.

All at once, her body slipped through a narrow hole in the veil and it dropped around her like a molted skin. She kicked it aside, and went to work on the others, teasing off a succession of purple, red, yellow, and orange veils, now and then flashing a hint of bare arm, or a jewel-encrusted, flesh-colored body suit that began at her breasts and ended who knows where. Her skin, even her body suit glowed with the rosy-pink color of health.

To take the veil

Every Catholic girl considers it at least once. The perceived romance of the nun's life is due half to its sacrifice, half to its habit. To "take the white" is to enter the novitiate; to "take the black" is to make one's final profession. A nun's veil is a reminder of her status as the bride of Christ, a symbol of her vows. To the dreamy young girl, it is suggestive of the hidden possibilities that may yet lie dormant in *her*—the promise of a vocation, a calling, a purpose. The thrill and terror that, at any moment, Christ might signal that he wishes to avail himself of her. Her desire to answer the call, to have a call to answer. To be chosen. To be loved and needed for her particular gifts. To be good, yes, to divest herself of the evils and uncertainties of the world once and for all.

*

The veil of St. Veronica

As Christ carried his cross on the road to Calvary, a woman gave him her veil to wipe his brow. The veil came away imprinted with the image of his face. The name "Veronica," as the woman came to be known, is a portmanteau of Latin and Greek: *vera ikon,* "true image." She is sometimes associated with the "Haemorrhissa," the woman in the Gospels who was "diseased with an issue of blood", or with a woman present at the beheading of John the Baptist, who collected drops of his blood.

Some say the veil was destroyed in the Sack of Rome in 1527, others that it may yet survive in the vaults of the Vatican.

Vestal Virgins

The Vestal Virgin is so named for her devotion to Vesta, goddess of the hearth. She stoked the Temple of Vesta's sacred fire and wore a white veil called a *suffibulum* as she performed her rituals. Vestal Virgins served for terms of thirty years and were expected to remain celibate for the duration of their service. If they broke their vow of chastity, their punishment was live burial. To draw the blood of a Vestal Virgin was forbidden.

*

Blood as a veil

To wear lipstick or to sweep blush on the apples of one's cheeks is to affect the appearance of blood. Pallor is a kind of frankness. A body drained of blood is a naked one.

In patients experiencing a significant bleeding event, a doctor or nurse may perform a preliminary assessment to determine the anemia's severity. In extreme cases, the patient's nailbeds will appear blue. The inside of the patient's lower eyelids will turn light pink or white. It may be difficult to locate a vein in the arm for further testing. When located, the patient may fear that the blood exiting her body is all she has left. She may beg you not to take any more. She may hallucinate a thousand tiny Rita Hayworths swirling into the test tube.

A shade

Waking up in the evening, I stumble out of bed, forgetting in my disorientation that I am not allowed to get up without calling for help. I walk to the bathroom, not bothering to turn on the light, my eyes permanently adjusted to darkness. When I wash my hands and look up at the mirror, I see a ghost—white, gaunt, with enormous sunken eyes. I start and fall backwards. The ghost falls with me.

Grandmother

The story goes that she brushed her hair, threw on her gown and a swipe of red lipstick, and drove to the church. There's such post-war self-sufficiency in her bearing, one hardly registers the veil, which doesn't rate for girlish softness and coquetry. It is fingertip-length and pencil-edged, and flares out slightly like the line of her square-necked New Look dress. She is gimlet-eyed, imploringly American, smiling—but a tad ironically, as if to say she usually favors a sweater set.

*

Widow's weeds

Most nights, she makes herself a dinner of tea and crackers, no longer able to stomach a big meal before bed. She nibbles before the cast of *Billions*. The only technology she can work is her DVR. She says she doesn't mind the solitude, says that sometimes in the past sixty years, she longed for it. But lately, yes, it has begun to wear.

Rita Hayworth as a veil

One Halloween, I stayed home dressed as Rita Hayworth. I painted my nails blood-red and applied such a quantity of rouge that my mother complained at the dent in her compact. I wore my great-aunt's floral halter dress over my listless white body. A father making the rounds with his son rang the doorbell, saw my nails as I handed out candy, and chastised me: "You're awfully young to be wearing such a grown-up color." I would have reddened if I could.

*

My body is a veil

In one of the two photographs taken of me during my illness, it is Christmas morning, and I seem to be made of marshmallow, propped up on a pile of pillows beside the tree. My eyes half-shut, I tug limply at the corner of a wrapped present, too far gone to know I am being photographed.

In the other, I am lingering in the background of a family scene and, in anticipation of the camera, hold up both hands to shield my face.

I came upon these photos in an album several years ago and tore them up.

St. Rita of Cascia

14th century Italian widow, later nun. She received the stigmata on her forehead in the form of a thorn from the crown of Christ. It created a wound that wept and bled for the rest of her life. The drops of blood from the wound were said to sparkle. She is typically depicted in a black veil, holding a rose, with a thorn in her forehead. She is the patron saint of many causes, among them blood disorders and gynecological problems.

*

The veil flutters

Drugs to stop the bleeding, though they never worked. Shots to send me into temporary menopause, to contract my uterus. Labor pains and hot flashes in the same year. Drugs to control the side effects of the other drugs. Not a girl, not a woman. Some third thing. Fast-forwarded through time, rewound when I needed to be. At once young and old, mature and pitifully naïve.

I convinced myself that only my mother and grandmother knew the full truth. They fed this delusion, whispering in the presence of my grandfather whenever we discussed anything too intimate, too revealing.

Then, on my thirteenth birthday, friends I hadn't seen in months came to look in, let slip that, at school, I was the object of daily speculation: pregnant, dead, something else they wouldn't say.

The Studio System

A Faustian bargain: in exchange for your freedom, a team of experts work to decode the cipher of your body. What silhouette suits your figure best? What shape should your eyes, lips, eyebrows be? Is the timbre of your voice tuned to comedy or drama? Once distilled to your essence, you are matched to a type, a role.

Now you need never wonder what kind of person you are, even if you were never certain, even if you look like no one in your family—not mother, grandmother, grandfather. Now you look like yourself. The veil inside you is lifted. Now all you must do is stay the same.

Black-Eyed Suzie's

My first regular gig. Of late an aging child prodigy,
now I sounded like a woman and was one.
"I don't know whether to take you over my knee
or take you over my knee," some barfly Cicero said.
("Why don't you think about it and get back to me?")
The microphone was somehow always wet,
the crowd forever three drinks deep. I thought
my classical training counted for something,
could bounce a textbook off my diaphragm,
belt an F5, sight-read anything. I liked to brag
that everyone I really dug was dead. Onstage,
hands folded, I nodded dutifully as the trumpet
player ran laps around "All the Things You Are"
and the rest of the guys walked offstage for
a Newport break. At last, our married bandleader
fired me because he "couldn't trust himself."
(He looked, for all the world, like a hardboiled egg.)
Sniffling, I packed my tote bag while the trumpet
player, that callous bastard, went on whistling
and polishing his horn. Ah, Suzie's. C'est la vie!

Voice Lessons

better now / stand up straight / stab at it
louder, louder / push from the / put your weight
too shy / Callas did / column of air
let the stomach / expand, contract / let the torso
accelerando / fill with air / repeat after
let the chest / stab at it / extend, extend
why Moffo / open throat / drop your jaw
if you listen / resist my hand / expand, contract
on your back / don't reach for / louder, louder
clean lines / repeat after / start your scales
push from the / as if a string / she used to say
column of air / on a sigh / Caballé was
support, support / expressivo / pure vowels
scale back / why Moffo / attack, attack
more legato / drop your jaw / open tone
too shy / she used to say / on a sigh
Callas did / now watch your / breathe, breathe
don't listen / Caballé wasn't / must be secco
as if a string / push from the / column of air

don’t reach for / let the stomach / no strain

good, fine / relax into the / take your time

better now / shoulders back / expand, contract

Salomé

Running Wilde's imagination was a wish
to see behind the curtain of Mark's prose,
in which he only noted that she "danced
to please King Herod's guests," then fixed a dish
served cold. Her charms (and how many she disclosed),
her need at last to catch the Baptist's glance
added flesh to Wilde's fabricated romance—

added scandal when, in an opera by Strauss
(its libretto lifted whole-cloth from the Wilde),
his star refused to strip down "like a whore."
She waited backstage, cross-armed in her blouse
while a ballerina, willing to go unveiled,
ran out to Herod's feet and covered for her,
then slipped behind the curtain like a metaphor.

Gallery Gods

It's a flat frontier city with something to prove:
the reinforced concrete tower on Wacker Drive,
the blood-colored CNA Tower that killed a woman.

The Tribune Tower (Rouen on protein shakes)
that flaunts its stash of noted rocks (Giza, Pompeii,
Westminster, Taj Mahal) like a man in a trenchcoat.

The Sears Tower (a Rock 'Em Sock 'Em Robot);
the Water Tower that stood in the Great Fire's char
like a kid hiding his hands behind his back (little squirt);

the Board of Trade Tower's 30-foot hood ornament:
a gunmetal Ceres, columnar but for the torpedo bra,
holding . . . an air rifle and a Monopoly money bag?

And you and I, in the very last row of the last gallery
of the Orchestra Hall, so high up, we can feel the change
slip from our pockets (you smother a laugh at my joke:

a red cocktail napkin to the nose), as we get our ears
boxed by Mahler—the fidgeting players, the choir
below us only dots—so that the Bean that bent us out

of shape, the Seurat that slayed us in the Art Institute
go vivid and recede, like a dream at altitude, and we
seem to be spinning on the pins of the Hancock Tower,

where earlier we eyed the vaporous rivers, watched the ice
roll out across the lake, spied Indiana, Michigan,
discussed the rate at which our soft pretzels might fall

("like thunderbolts"). So it seemed that, there in the Hall,
I suddenly understood optimism, or at least the winged
exhilaration of the enterprise, this waging a vertical war

on a windy plain, as we bumped our heads on the white lid of the ceiling, and the timpani of the "Resurrection Symphony" pounded out their final notes of paradise.

Doppler Effect

The siren surges like a swarm of bees
that synchronize the minds within their hive—
a cartoon tide that's winding up to sting
an unsuspecting mark—or like a swing
in one unending uptick, pumping knees
advancing to the sky, till it arrives

and rolls out, like a gurney, its true sound:
a range leashed in by one recurring pitch
in even-crested, evenly troughed waves
that you can almost see. Rolling waves
or canopies of firmly-tethered sound
that seem so deeply lodged until the pitch,

released to rarefaction, pulls away.
In chords of taffy, stretched out to nadir,
the siren slips and plummets down the scale.
Its sharp notes turned to flat, the rolling tail
of its long scarf of sound reduced to sway,
it vanishes below what you can hear.

Bel Canto

> "Is it raining, is it snowing outside La Scala? Who cares."
> —Stendhal

It was the mouth of Callas,
        la grande bouche nestled below
a Greek-pediment nose,

and I was there inside it:
        the stalls comprising the mass
of a shifting tongue,

the boxes a triple set of square
        and gritted teeth (the *loggionisti*
clamoring like toothaches),

the proscenium's red folds
        a pharynx, portal to the arias
throbbing in her throat—

Anna Bolena mourning for her
        faded star, a masked stranger
revealing her Borgia name

on the terrace of a palazzo,
        Amina crying in her sleep
as she crosses the high mill bridge . . .

And the dome of the ceiling,
        with its white plasterwork ridges,
was the roof of her mouth

(though Legge reported its shape
        was a Gothic arch, bowed as
a wishbone, sharp as the Duomo's,

tunneling its point down
        to the soft palate's transept, thus
accounting for its "veiled" sound),

from which a chandelier-
        uvula dangles like a grace note,
shimmering in the void,

above the crowd, the stage,
        the singers who are not she
and never could be, but

move within her, like worshippers
        in a nave or words to a melody,
formed of thought and air.

Vocal Collapse

> "If I cannot sing, I have the impression that I no longer exist."
> —Montserrat Caballé

Somewhere else, someone is taking up Vaccai,
waking up her voice like a child for school.
It leaps out of bed, flexes without cursing,
too young, too simple to disobey commands,
and performs what older voices cannot do
because it doesn't know what can't be done.

You can hear her on the stair, singing solfege,
straight-toned, faceless as an empty spoon.
Soon, she'll dream of marbles in her mouth,
of a sore throat that won't cure, of the Malebolge
where the diviners circle, heads backwards,
necks twisted in a pose forbidding sound.

It will start with age, with a push, with the thrill
of pain for a note that reaches higher, higher
again—and for five years, maybe ten, the voice,
bruised into renown, will shake the hearer
from his seat, will flush with held-off disaster,
until by doing, doing more, it comes undone.

Avail

(continued)

Thinning of the veil

Through the wall, my grandmother hears two people speaking softly. She wonders how visitors could have entered the house unnoticed, goes into my grandfather's bedroom to see who they are. He is alone and asleep. Later, he tells her that a man and a woman stood beside his bed, discussing his failing heart and the state of his soul. He assures her that he does not feel afraid.

*

Superior/anterior medullary velum

The veil of the brain. A layer of white matter stretched between the cerebellum and mid-brain, forming the "roof" of the fourth ventricle. It is so thin as to be translucent. Its function is not yet fully understood.

Fibrin

Damage to a blood vessel triggers a two-step clotting response. In primary hemostasis, platelets, with the aid of a glycoprotein known as the von Willebrand factor, adhere to each other to form a plug in the breach. Secondary hemostasis consists of the "coagulation cascade," in which a protein called fibrin weaves a loose web around the plug to hold it in place, trapping red and white blood cells in its lacing to form a clot or thrombus. Clotting factors activate to harden the fibrin's tendrils into a stiff veil.

A patient with insufficient clotting or von Willebrand factors is said to suffer from hemophilia or von Willebrand's disease. Such conditions are marked by an inferior clotting response or the total inability to form a clot. The patient may be prone to uncontrollable external or internal bleeding.

*

Thrombophilia

A patient who forms clots too readily is said to suffer from thrombophilia. Danger arises if the veil of a clot detaches from the vessel wall and enters the blood stream, whereupon it may block the flow of a vein or artery. Pulmonary embolism, in which blood clots travel to and reside in the lungs, causes death or a host of serious conditions. In many patients, the increased pressure in the lungs puts undue strain on the heart, commonly resulting in heart failure.

In a hospital in New Haven, Connecticut, a cardiologist told his patient that there may be a genetic link between thrombophilia and hemophilia. He was not surprised to hear that his patient had a granddaughter with a bleeding disorder.

The veil as metaphor

In Bernini's sculpture, *Truth Unveiled by Time,* Truth is a little hippy and carries an extra roll of fat on her gut. No one looks good naked, my mother once told me. Once the shock value wears off, you long for a fig leaf, a pair of panties, a sandwich board—a little boundary of dignity between you and the bare necessities. Sure, she looks thrilled now, even ecstatic to be seen for what she is. But time has a way of turning pleasure stale. Eventually, she'll realize she's caught a chill.

*

The veil as fabrication

She has stripped for me, for innumerable doctors, for the parade of visiting nurses. Still, she will not look in the mirror. She stands in the back room of the house, beside a table strewn with informational packets from the breast surgeon, the plastic surgeon, the oncologist, the radiologist, with spools of bandages, with individually-wrapped gauze pads, with creams and ointments, with diagrams, with compression garments of various sizes, and watches me as, twice daily, I unwrap her, using my face for her mirror. She can't be comforted. When I help her change for bed, she takes off her glasses so she won't catch an accidental glimpse in the vanity. When at last she can shower on her own, she does not look down.

To lift the veil

See also: an unveiling. I bid goodbye to any notions I've cherished of grace or mystery. I see things as they really are, which is to say, I see that things are plain and dull and affectless. I see that they are flat, flatter than I thought they might be, and stretching onwards to a vanishing point with an astounding frankness and banality. Flat like the plains of Nebraska or Kansas, flat as a sentence without irony. There are no bends in the road, no wrinkles in time. This is the way things are, the way they will be.

*

A vale

A few years ago, a body in a state of considerable decay was discovered by a hiker in City Creek Canyon. Experts could neither identify the body nor establish a cause of death. No one knew how long the body had been lingering in the vale, though it had likely gone undetected for many weeks. The steep hillsides, keeping the secret of the body's provenance, buried their heads in the snow.

Mother

The Princess Di fad ran long—a style, like the bulk of 80s fashion, that you now deem romantic and revivalist, an association of big hair and big dresses with big feeling. It was an era of optimism, security, generosity towards the past: Merchant Ivory, *Back to the Future,* Madonna. And you, the spitting image of Marisa Tomei, in a gown whose sleeves have sleeves, whose veil-headband is itself adorned with a frosting of little white tendrils reaching into your shoulder-length, teased hair. As you hold up a glass of champagne, a breeze catches your veil, and it is hard not to think of royalty, Disney or otherwise, in the fantasia of that little moment, the magic balance of profusion on the wing.

The mask vs. the veil

A mask is typically decorated to depict a human or animal head. It is a pretense, a front intended to disguise or deceive. It provides an alternate face.

A veil is a covering designed to screen, shield, decorate, or circumscribe. Its pretense takes the form of a blank. A veil allows two options at once: positive and negative, self and non-self. It both covers and highlights the body.

The mask indulges the desire to hide, even behind a facsimile of one's own face. The mask may slip, or it may not; to see behind the mask is an unexpected privilege. The veil, by its nature, creates a need for revelation. While one might wonder what is beneath the mask, one must wonder what is beneath the veil.

The mask is usually static. It hides the contours of the face, head, body. The veil is viscous, fluid, elastic, elusive.

The mask is narrative. The veil is lyric.

To cast/throw/draw a veil (over)

Your work does not contain the necessary self-revelation. The list of things you'd rather not say is long; the passion play of your life, however blood-soaked, fails to find the page. You skirt the issues. You are cagey, skittish, untrusting. You lack the necessary interest even in self-preservation.

You claim to reveal yourself by hiding in your interests, say that the shape of your preoccupations forms the outline of a body. But haven't you heard that discretion is no longer a virtue?

*

I have to tell you

how much I hate them. I can't permit myself to wear so much as a flounce for fear I might be flaunting something. I can't forget the ways my body has betrayed me. I can't forget the girl in the photograph, swollen and white, so unlike the olive-skinned brides that lined the walls of my mother's house. I hate the veil for the pleasure the wearer must take in her body—a pleasure I can't feel.

The veil of paint

Manet's veil destroys. His "Young Woman" wears a veil with a black-lace trim that streaks across her lips in a zigzag band like a jack-o-lantern—or a corpse with its mouth sewn shut.

In Monet's "Camille on the Beach in Trouville," Camille wears a transparent veil which bunches its silver gauze beneath her nose like the tube of an oxygen tank.

Roslin's "Lady with the Veil" holds her black satin mantle across her face so that it occludes her right eye. The veil has plucked it out.

*

A curtain

I was the last person to see him alive. It was the end of visiting hours, and I had spent the day beside his bed, holding his hand, encouraging him to eat although he hadn't yet opened his eyes. When I told him it was time for me to go, he lifted one hand, black-brown from the butterfly needles inserted into his thick veins, and brought a finger to his cheek, signaling for a kiss. I kissed him, told him I would see him tomorrow, opened the blue-and-white privacy curtain around his bed, and left without a thought. When I walked through the door of my mother's house, she was on the phone with hospice. They called to say that he had died a few minutes after I left his room.

The uncanny valley

The digital rendering of a too-lifelike humanoid, or the post-production addition of prosthetics to the human face or form, causes diminished sympathies or even revulsion in the viewer. The nearer an animated human in a film or video game approaches aesthetic congruity to our own faces, the more we identify with and love it—until we do not. At the point of uncanny likeness, human "affinity" for the face made in our image drops precipitously. Most often the problem is something in the eyes, an eerie coldness or an artificial spark. Some veil remains between what is real and what is false. A technological boundary remains to be crossed.

*

Funeral shroud

At my grandfather's open-casket wake, I stayed in the adjoining room, unable to cross the threshold and view the body. My aunt negotiated with me over the course of the viewing as if I was holding myself hostage, trying to appeal to the part of me that was sane. Finally, she convinced me with a whisper: "It doesn't look like him. Pretend it isn't." Inside was a body bearing no relation to anyone I knew. The distance between his nose and upper lip dragged on like a lie. I touched the hem of his suit, then watched my grandmother slip a few ancient homemade cards into his hand. "Dear Grandpa," ran the childish handwriting which, I am told, was once mine.

Beyond the veil

Sometimes I think I see him on the street. Once I followed a man in Boston for five extra blocks, just to be sure. They wore the same coat, had the same gait. I was just waiting for the right time to surprise you, he might say. Did you ever think I'd really leave you? Death is not a veil, but a wall. This is the only impassable, the only cruel idiom.

Road Trip Sestina

Across and down, we take the country's measure
like a seamstress fitting a woman for a dress.
Beside me, my mother, a pillow on her chest,
maps out each road and highway, stitch by stitch.
Neither of us has driven through the West, crossed
the mountains rippling the continent's wide veil,

seen the Badlands, the Tetons, the waterfalled vales
out of Bierstadt. At night in our hotel, we measure
two kinds of progress: she, marking guidebooks, crossing
off names; I, surveying the skin beneath her dressing,
changing bandages, checking every pale stitch
that snakes from her sides to the middle of her chest,

strewing stained coffee tables and plywood chests
with wrappers. The cancer looked like a veil,
the doctors said, a sheet of lacework stitched
through the tissue. (They took "extreme measures.")
I lay out her clothes for tomorrow, then help her dress
for bed, putting aside her scapular and cross.

When she returns home, flies back alone across
the country (TSA wands beeping over her chest),
she'll have to face her new body, take her dresses
to a friend, a seamstress, to see if she might veil
the loss with fabric, or else take measurements
for custom clothes. She'll cry at not having a stitch

to wear . . . But for now, she indulges my itch
for travel, wants to think only of the next cross-
road, of the nearest park entrance, of measuring
me against the world's-largest-something, of The Hope Chest,
where she hopes to find "cowboy gear" (to no avail)
and I model a 70's sheath just like a dress

she once wore. Soon, we'll punch in the address
of our last stop, drive a highway that stitches
over the ribs of the Wasatch, its peaks veiled
in smoke that falls to the valley floor, and cross
into Salt Lake—my street the lowest drawer in the chest
of the hillside. My mother tries to reassure me,

tugging at her cross, that she feels better. Her chest
hardly hurts anymore. Her stitches freshly dressed,
she says goodbye in a voice measured but veiled.

The Phoenicians

Transplants both, like the palm trees
that lend the landscape a tropical legibility,
they live in an invented place,
precarious as language.

Squat, blank, rectangular, their house admits
nothing, forms a single brick in a wall
just one brick tall. All the neighbors seem
to make a living in encryption.

Their little boy can't learn the word for "cloud,"
but knows "camel," "cactus," "dee-doo"—
his name for the bird that hovers
over the dryscaping,

looking for a place to land. I walk him by the canal
that runs its concrete vein through Scottsdale,
feeds the pool at the Arizona Biltmore,
where once, in a deck chair,

Irving Berlin dreamt up "White Christmas"
over a Tequila Sunrise, fighting the dual
oppressions of happiness and heat.
Who wouldn't long for snow,

for history, for an end to the inveterate blinking
of the neon signs that flash their native terms:
"Domino's," and, just beneath it, "Guns."
But at dusk, the sky runs

Tyrian purple, and the saguaros on the hills
throw their inscrutable alphabet-shadows
across serifs of agave—a living document,
vigorous and prickly.

Andermatt

The hamlet grew up the wall of the valley
like a tubercule. I kept dreaming of suffocation.
By day, the streets had the uncanny vacancy
of a model train village. Every fifteen minutes
a Protestant and a Catholic church tolled
their Kappel War of mutual headaches.
Shopkeepers had no patience with me.
The river, indifferent, reflected nothing.
I secretly hoped for some magic to happen
but hedged against it, sitting in my hotel,
reading Mann, yawning. I watched a film
with Isabelle Huppert, a bad one, in which
she plays a professor with some problem—
a nebulous flaw like remoteness or frigidity.
She takes her wisp of a body to a chalet
to smoke weed and talk garbage philosophy
with a hot young thing she doesn't even kiss . . .
Next morning, the usual caravans circled
the ski lifts, let off tourists in search of
altitude, fortitude, après ski, while the peaks,
snow-capped as 8-balls, kept their distance,
went on with the sturdy work of aspiration.
Huppert sobers up, departs for Paris, thinks
to herself, *Why not?* or else, *Who cares?*
I stayed behind, still waiting for the answer.

Italian Triptych

I. Good Friday

Dear S.—What a time to be abroad.
Closed are the Doge's Palace, the Guggenheim,
and La Fenice, on whose cracked façade
I scraped my shin pretending to wait in line.
Some joke. Even the Bridge of Sighs
is boarded up (*Lavori in corso!*)
with car ads and a water-stained blue sky.
Come three, no admittance to San Marco—
white-haired bouncers, sighing "*turista*,"
turned me away. (My Neapolitan's
worth peanuts here.) Skipping a siesta,
I watched a sunburnt couple feed the pigeons
and get chewed out by a cop. (It's illegal.)
"They're fasting," I said, "but try the seagulls."

II. Holy Saturday

Exiled to the Loggia dei Lanzi,
I sit beside the *leoni dei Medici*
and contemplate the David
(well, its outdoor copy), obligated
to find it great. And so it is . . . Oh, S.,
I'd love to see Forster's Florence,
or the Firenze that broke Michelangelo's nose.
In mine it rains. A man's face glows
by the light of his phone (the nouveau Baedeker),
then—click—he is a clocklike selfie-sticker,
turning his back to me on the hour. Yawning,
one blasé kitty beneath our awning
(a far cry from the winged Venetian genus—

this one, sans gospel, is a humanist)
toys with the bocce ball in his paw,
where time has written lewd scrimshaw,
and dreams of meat. He eyes the trophy
Perseus parts from a contorted body—
its superfluous grape-bunched blood, the curl
of its skin like a wrinkled collar,
its full lips . . . Selfie man walks past and spits
at a Sabine's feet. A pigeon takes a shit
on horse-sick Cosimo. In the glowering dark,
deeper still for being outside the arc
of a floodlight, the Palazzo stands (mammoth
cubicle!), its castellated tower toothed
and black. Stone cold, I start for my *pensione*.
The Duomo's pitted face is Fabergé.
The Baptistry's mum as a puzzle box,
just waiting for heaven to be unlocked.

III. Easter Sunday

Not morning Mass outside the Vatican
(a dead ringer for the Last Judgment—or so
I imagine, only having seen the fresco
secondhand), nor the campy Trevi Fountain,
with its faux Anita Ekbergs and con men,
the Mouth of Truth (a drain), Via Veneto,
nor lunch, when out of my pizza dough
a spider sprang like Christ from an open
tomb—nothing could (forgive me) resurrect
this Roman holiday . . . that is, until
I stumbled on the Forum (free), its Temple
of Saturn a winking portcullis (the architect
of ruins hates a door)—or just a sash and lintel,
with a view, dear S., that made me thank the rubble.

Going South

after *Italian Hours*

At long last, this was my reward: a dream
come to life along the Bay of Naples,
its golden nook at the summery extreme
from my cold trek across northern steeples.

Off the bay's far bend stood the Isle of Capri,
concealed in shadow—Naples's sly mistress,
but when approached, a mountain on the sea,
lime-white excepting a trim of citrus.

Far aloft on the great rocks was pitched,
as the first note of a wondrous concert,
the town of Anacapri, whose sight bewitched
all comers with her antique glamour. Her skirt

of shady loggias and sunny canopies
belled out around a quiet square,
at whose center, under rows of balconies,
stood a fountain licking at the hot air.

I sat on its edge a long afternoon,
observing *passeggiatas* on the hour.
Above and below was brightest blue,
till evening fell like a black flower.

March 27

The foothills still white-headed, I turn
to the cemetery for exercise, taking laps
around its numbered streets—orderly,

wide, apathetic. On a few polished
stones, the second dates are not yet carved.
I'm thinking of the spring I played Evita,

how my second-act hair was sprayed
blonde as limestone, and my health
failed through several late numbers.

How I died and was embalmed onstage,
laid in a glass casket and paraded past
a chorus of mourners. I remember

pinching my thigh, trying not to laugh.
But you left, I heard later, waited
in the lobby, tearful, till the curtain fell.

On or off stage, I was always playing
dead, taking close calls as lightly, yes,
as curtain calls. You—*paisan*, of hearty

mountain-stock—made no provisions
for your funeral, conceived of yourself
as an eternal gardener, the displaced squire

of the olive trees in your village, yielding
oil for the Palace of Caserta's long table
years after the kingdom's collapse.

Now, on your birthday, I can't fathom
having survived you. Thousands of miles
away, a palm cross rustles on your grave.

The Gold of Naples

Things kept reminding me of other things.
The old ladies in the street were my aunts.
A counterman at Caffè Mexico
was Totò in a soda fountain hat.
The rum babas were trumpet mutes.
My hanging Moka pots were little men
with barrel-of-monkeys arms. This garden
looked like Barcelona, that piazza
was a picture of a picture of Rome.
Vesuvius was a Crawford eyebrow
arched over the bay. My pizza oven
of an apartment was—it really was—
the apartment in *The Gold of Naples,*
and I was me, or some baked and dusky
version of myself, and I was alone
and half-delirious and overweight.
An Aussie tourist by a book stall turned
to me and said, "Those Japanese experts
say this place will blow at any moment.
If you thought Pompeii was trouble"—I did—
"just wait." From my roof I watched the sunset
through a bottle of Strega, and it was
a John Martin painting, one of those camp
apocalyptic bugaboos. Now how
does the saying go? Resemblances are
just the shadows of differences . . . The end
of my world is the beginning of yours.

NOTES

This book's epigraph is taken from Anne Carson's translation of Fragment 100 in *If Not, Winter: Fragments of Sappho.*

"Avail" is greatly indebted to Anne Carson's *Eros the Bittersweet,* particularly her discussion of aīdos in the chapter, "Tactics." Additionally, many sections within "Avail" were informed and enriched by outside sources, listed below in order of appearance:

> Information and quotes in "*The flammeum*" were drawn from the chapter "The Costume of the Roman Bride" by Laetitia La Follette in *The World of Roman Costume,* edited by Judith Lynn Sebesta and Larissa Bonfante, and from the entry for "nubile" in the *Oxford English Dictionary.*
>
> "*Cumulonimbus velum*" was informed by the entries for "accessory cloud" and "velum" in the *Glossary of Meteorology* at the American Meteorological Society's website (glossary.ametsoc.org).
>
> "*Palatal velum*" is indebted to the *Encyclopedia Britannica*'s entry on the "soft palate" and the chapter "The English Nasal Consonants" in *An Outline of English Phonetics* (9th edition) by Daniel Jones.
>
> Details on invasive lobular carcinoma were gathered from Mayo Clinic hand-outs provided to my mother.
>
> "*Velum [mycology]*" was informed by the chapter on "Homobasidiomycetes" in *Introduction to Fungi* (3rd edition) by John Webster and Roland W. S. Weber.
>
> Information in "*The veil of St Veronica*" was found in the entry on "St. Veronica" on the *Catholic Encyclopedia*'s website

(www.newadvent.org/cathen). Quoted material on the bleeding woman is from Matthew 9:20–22 (KJV).

"Vestal Virgins" draws upon the *World History Encyclopedia* and the *Encyclopedia Britannica*'s entries on "Vestal Virgins." Information on the "suffibulum" was found in "The Costume of the Roman Bride" by Laetitia La Follette in *The World of Roman Costume,* edited by Judith Lynn Sebesta and Larissa Bonfante.

"Superior/anterior medullary velum" was informed by the section "The Hind-brain or Rhombencephalon" in *Gray's Anatomy* (20th edition).

Information in *"Fibrin"* was found in the Encyclopedia Britannica's entry on "bleeding and blood clotting." *"Thrombophilia"* draws upon the entry on "thrombophilia" at the Cleveland Clinic Health Library's website (my.clevelandclinic.org/health).

Information and quotes in *"The uncanny valley"* were found in "The Uncanny Valley" by Masahiro Mori (originally published in the journal *Energy* in 1970), translated by Karl F. MacDorman and Norri Kageki and published in *IEEE Spectrum* on June 12, 2012. Also helpful was an essay on Mori's theory, "What Is the Uncanny Valley? Creepy robots and the strange phenomenon of the uncanny valley: definition, history, examples, and how to avoid it" by Rina Diane Caballar, published November 6, 2019 in *IEEE Spectrum.*

"A vale" references the article "Human remains found in canyon near Salt Lake City" by the Associated Press, published in the *Salt Lake Tribune* on April 27, 2020.

"The mask vs. the veil" was informed by the entries on "mask" and "veil" in the *Oxford English Dictionary.*

The epigraph to "Bel Canto" is my own loose translation of a line in Stendhal's *Rome, Naples, and Florence.*

"Road Trip Sestina" is for my mother.

"Pacific Palisades" takes inspiration from Susan Sontag's 1987 essay "Pilgrimage" in *The New Yorker* and Lara Feigel's *The Bitter Taste of Victory: Life, Love and Art in the Ruins of the Reich,* which records Mann's conversation with Herman Hesse.

"The Phoenicians" is for Patrick Fox and his mother, Hannah.

"In the Morgan Library" is for Ange Mlinko.

"Italian Triptych" is for Sadie Hoyt.

ACKNOWLEDGMENTS

Grateful acknowledgment is made to the editors of the publications where these poems first appeared:

32 Poems: "A Childhood Illness," "Doppler Effect"

32 Poems Emerging Poet Feature: "Snow," "Cover Girl," "Bel Canto"

AGNI: "The Awful Truth"

Bad Lilies: "Andermatt," "Skyscrapers," "In the Morgan Library"

Bridport Prize Anthology 2023: "Road Trip Sestina"

The Los Angeles Review: "The Gold of Naples," "St. Catherine's Wheel," "Vocal Collapse" (as "Elegy")

The New Criterion: "The Swing"

Nimrod: "For Frances Gumm," "His Girl Friday"

The Southern Review: "High Culture" (reprinted on the Academy of American Poets website)

Subtropics: "Black-Eyed Suzie's," "Gallery Gods," "Italian Triptych," "Marriage," "Oxford," "The Phoenicians," "Salomé"

The Yale Review: "Pacific Palisades"

Boundless gratitude to Nicholas Pierce, Marie McGrath, Allison Field Bell, Jasmine Khaliq, Chengru He, and all my friends at the Universities of Florida and Utah for their generous help, talent, encouragement, and laughter.

I'm enormously thankful to the professors and mentors whose wisdom, guidance, and support made this book possible, especially

Katharine Coles, Paisley Rekdal, Rick Barot, Richard Preiss, Vincent Cheng, William Logan, and Michael Hofmann.

Love to Ange Mlinko for everything. Love to my family, especially my sister, Riley, and my mother, Lynne.

Erin O'Luanaigh worked as a jazz singer before receiving her MFA in Poetry from the University of Florida. Her poems have appeared in *The Yale Review, AGNI, The Southern Review, 32 Poems, Bad Lilies, Subtropics, Nimrod, The Hopkins Review,* and elsewhere. She is currently a Steffensen Cannon Fellow at the University of Utah. *Avail* is her first book.

photo by Riley O'Luanaigh

Ange Mlinko is the author of seven books of poetry, most recently *Foxglovewise,* and a book of lyric criticism, *Difficult Ornaments: Florida and the Poets.* She has won the Randall Jarrell Award in Criticism, the Frederick Bock Prize, and a Guggenheim Fellowship. She is a frequent contributor to the *New York Review of Books* and the *London Review of Books,* and teaches poetry at the University of Florida, where she directs the MFA program.